Copyright©2012 HONEY Ventures, Inc.

ISBN: 978-0-615-60379-7

All rights reserved. No part of this book may be reproduced in any form by any electronic or mechanical means including photocopying, recording, or information storage and retrieval without permission in writing from the author unless proper reference is given following each statement used or for the sole intent of classroom use.

Printed in the USA

I AM A Leader of Now

Nathan Burrell

Contents

The Pledge	5
Author's note	6
Foreword	8

Chapters

Introduction	14
1 Leader of Now	18
2 Dream Now	30
3 Passion Now	43
4 Decide Now	50
5 Plan Now	59
6 Act Now	67
Leaders of Now	73
Jovan	74
Robert	80
Sean	84
Marissa	86
Clinton	90
Rayna	93
The principles	97

The Project Pledge

I am a person with passion, drive and vision. I am a world changer and a *leader of now*. As an entrepreneur I operate at the highest level of integrity and honesty. The world's wealth is entrusted in my hands. Therefore, I use profit to provide for my needs, empower others and defend the poor.

Helping Our Nations Empowering Youth Project Pledge

Author's Note

There are so many worthy causes to support and so many people in need. It can seem a bit overwhelming when you sit down and think about the challenges that are facing our local communities, cities, states and nations. So, where do we begin? How can we help, let alone make a real difference?

I might not have the answer to cure the problems that we all face, especially our youth, but I do have a suggestion that can have a major impact on you and those around you…Lead Now! The concept of Leader of Now became clear to me as I began to notice more and more people "*talk*" about what they wanted to do, or how they wanted to help, but still waiting on some future event to happen in their life before they did anything at all. I also wanted a way to encourage the youth that we work with to get involved now. When I wrote the Project Pledge, an affirmation to remind me, our students and those we serve what the HONEY Project is all about, the declaration: I Am A Leader of Now became that call to action.

I pray this book will challenge you to re-think your definition of success and stir up the passion inside of you not only to *talk* about the problems, but to take action now. This is not a follow me manual or a secret to success book, but simple words of encouragement and permission to start dreaming again.

By the way, you just became a Leader of Now! By supporting this book, 50% of the proceeds is going to support the Helping Our Nations Empowering Youth Project (HONEY Project) www.honeyproject.org to help young people address the issues of extreme poverty and youth empowerment through social enterprise. So there, I have already helped you do something great. Now the rest is up to you.

Improving Lives Couldn't Be Sweeter!

Nathan Burrell
Agogo, Ghana 2011

FOREWARD

Back in 1984 when I was only 18 years old I told my dad that I wanted to convert my volunteer work into a paying job so I could bootstrap my way into the future, travel the world, and help connect people, resources, and ideas to improve the quality of life for others around the globe. My dad who is a family physician told me earnestly to simply stay in college and prepare to become one of tomorrow's leaders. Over the years life consisted of a cycle. Go to work, volunteer, go to school, go to church, and care for my family.

Time flew past and soon the belief that social enterprise was a plausible concept dissipated from my immediate memory. However, on a late Thursday afternoon in 2010 I received an email which rekindled my belief that the two concepts could possibly co-exist perfectly. The communication simply let me know that the sender had located a youth centered social entrepreneurism program, in response to my inquiry, and disclosed that it was in the same county as my office.

I intently read the lines several times and learned that the HONEY Project (Helping Our Nations Empowering Youth) was a recommended youth program which had a visionary at the helm named Nathan Burrell. The email further shared that the company's founder would be presenting at Florida Atlantic University (FAU) that Saturday so I hurriedly sent off an email to R.S.V.P., left a voicemail of interest, prepared my elevator speech of our need, and re-arranged my busy work and volunteer schedule to visit the "HONEY" class at FAU that Saturday.

I anxiously awaited Saturday's event and when I arrived Mr. Burrell was about to welcome the youth and usher them into their first week of the 12 week journey to become "Change Agents." It was clear within the first ten minutes of our introductions that this man of God was genuinely on a mission to make a difference in the world. The room was literally buzzing with excitement as youth between 15 and 24 from different ethnic and socio-economic groups came together to hear what a social entrepreneur is and determine how they could become one.

As the youth listened to the HONEY alumni speak the room become electric. Within the twinkling of an eye it became clear when Nathan spoke again that he was empowering the youth to become Leaders of Now and he had been blessed and commissioned with a special gift to educate, uplift, and empower others. Like the budding change agents in the room I was swept up by his energy and passion to help alleviate global poverty and encourage economic development.

I decided immediately that I would not only ask him to partner with me to help the youth in my program where I worked but that I would also volunteer and fully support HONEY. That day began my journey of recognizing that I had been a social entrepreneur for so many years, like the students Nathan effortlessly shepherded in his programs, and that I was not only a change agent but had been a leader of now….back then.

Since the moment I met Nathan Burrell it was clear that The HONEY Project was not simply a job for him, but it was a movement of change. As a pillar in the community he had excelled in business both as an entrepreneur and member of several noteworthy corporate structures. I have watched Nathan tirelessly teach youth here and abroad about business and social enterprise and have been moved as he and his wonderful wife Jacquecine and four beautiful children opened their hearts and gently help provide guidance to those traveling into the fullness of their blessings.

I Am A Leader of Now is not simply a coffee table book or the compilation of a few "feel good" stories about youth in America who are helping people in Africa or other underdeveloped nations. It is a book which demonstrates how empowered youth have generated innovative ideas, maximized the resources available, and worked collaboratively worldwide to alleviate poverty by harnessing the power of people, passion, planet, and profit.

This amazing book will definitely move readers to action because it captures the essence of the social entrepreneurism movement and provides specific directions to help elevate and empower those who read it and have a desire to affect change.

Ultimately, our lives are shaped by our decisions and this book can serve as a reference for change. I want to close by simply thanking Nathan Burrell. As a colleague and friend thanks to you my bucket list runneth over and Improving Lives Couldn't be Sweeter.

Today my life's work has a name and I have been blessed to be a member of HONEY. I definitely encourage readers to treat themselves to this wonderful book and delight in the warmth, wisdom, and wonder that you will receive when you read I Am A Leader of Now.

Be Blessed!

Teresa D. Patterson
HONEY Ventures, Inc., Vice President and COO
Director/Co-founder of HONEY Project Academy of Technology and Social Enterprise

"We live in an age when to be young and to be indifferent can be no longer synonymous. We must prepare for the coming hour. The claims of the future are represented by suffering millions; and the youth of a nation are the trustees of prosperity." Benjamin Disraeli

INTRODUCTION

It's 9:30am on a Saturday morning and the room was filled with energetic students, a little more excited than usual as this was the point in their training where they would choose their company name. For the next 12 weeks these 20 or so students would be called by the name they picked this day for the duration of their time in the Academy. I tried my best to keep up with the brainstorming session as they shouted name after name for me to write on the whiteboard.

Future World Changers...Leaders of Tomorrow...Future Business Owners...Future Leaders Club...

The list went on and on inevitably with some variation of the word future in it. Finally, through the process of elimination, they settled on the name Leaders of Tomorrow. Then, all of a sudden, one young man stood up at his seat and walked to the front of the room and looked me straight in the eye and said: "Mr. Burrell, I can't wait until tomorrow, I need to make something happen today". Then he turned to his fellow students and encouraged them to change the name from tomorrow to today. Needless to say, Leaders of Today became the official name of that student class.

His words of "making something happen today" never left me, and over the years I began to notice this "future" mindset that so many of our youth subscribe to like they are waiting for something to happen to them instead of being the catalyst of change. Therefore, this book is intended to be a timeless, inspirational guide to assist readers young and the young at heart alike that can't wait until tomorrow and have the desire of becoming a leader of now. The truth is, each day and in every generation, the opportunity will always present itself for leaders of now to reveal themselves to invent, innovate, and solve some of society's most challenging issues no matter where they persist or for how long.

Unfortunately, in a well-meaning attempt to protect the youth from current problems or ills, we have called them the "future" unwittingly preventing them from doing something extraordinary, and disengaging them from what's happening and affecting them right now. By labeling the youth our future, we have subconsciously told them to wait for some point in time beyond an actual moment that invites them to get involved now.

Social rhetoric has made the youth indifferent, but emerging technology has made them relevant.

We live in an age where news of an uprising, global crises, or important cause can go viral through social networks and instantaneously downloaded to smart phones all over the world, and can no longer be hidden from the youth of today. In each of these situations or challenges that we may face as a society, therein, presents the opportunity for the youth to be bold, daring, inventive perhaps even heroic.

However, I believe a paradigm shift is underway as society and industry recognizes the opportunity not only to engage youth in dialogue, but to seek their participation in solving some of those formidable issues through social enterprise and innovation.

I Am A Leader of Now is a rallying cry to the youth, a motivational plea, an invitation to get involved now and not wait for some distant destination or moment in the future. Society needs you now. Benjamin Disraeli once said: "The youth of a Nation are the trustees of prosperity." Therefore, through a collaborative effort, today's youth must be empowered to develop new models and effectively utilize innovation to address societal gaps and stimulate economic development. If there is going to be any "future" prosperity to be trustees over, it must be created by the Leaders of Now.

1
LEADER OF NOW

THE NOW

What are you waiting for? Graduation? A diploma? A degree? A raise? The corner office? Money? Let me guess, some mysterious moment in the future when your ship comes in. Sorry to burst your bubble but it rarely happens that way. Pursuing your purpose, success or fulfilling your dreams in any endeavor happens when people take action. Those that are successful at accomplishing anything meaningful do 5 essential things: they dream big, they have passion, they make a decision, they plan and then they act. Perhaps they had a God given dream, or a vision that revealed their purpose. Inspired by that dream to accomplish their purpose, every decision and step they made was well orchestrated to get them closer to the fulfillment of that dream.

No matter what the motivation you must decide to do something now. Choose to live not just for the moment or even in the moment, but rather allow each moment to present opportunities for you to take action and lead now. In other words, allow each challenge, problem, injustice or circumstance to provide you with an opportunity to live with passion by using your God given abilities to do something awesome and fulfill your purpose. True *change agents* have a desire to see transformation not only in themselves but in the communities they live and eventually the world. We all tend to put things off in the future as an excuse and usually nothing gets done. Therefore, I use the term "now" as a way of remaining diligent and passionate about today with the intent of impacting your future. I like the way Phil Keoghan's book "NOW" defines it-No Opportunities Wasted.

There are some things that you will do or doing now that won't manifest until some point in the future. But that doesn't mean you stop doing what you need to do now. For example, you go to school every day only to receive a diploma in the future, or you go to work every day to receive a future check. But you don't stop going to school or work, because if you did you won't get that diploma and you don't get that check.

Whatever you're doing or not doing now will absolutely affect your future. Unfortunately, the problem has been too much of the future mindset which breeds procrastination, especially when you're young. This deferment of action and putting off until tomorrow is what I believe leads to the indifference Disraeli speaks about in his quote: "we live in an age when to be young and indifferent can no longer be synonymous." You may have thought the term "youth" provided you with a license to be cavalier about the issues society is facing today, but let me remind you of the fact that the unresolved issues you ignore today will be the very same issues you face tomorrow.

There will never be a right time and there is no piece of paper or special occasion that can qualify you as ready to make a difference. So, why not make a decision to get involved now, this very moment to impact the world. Deliberate and committed action is the primary requisite for potential leaders of now.

LEADERS

"As we look ahead into the next century, leaders will be those who empower others."

Bill Gates

"A true leader must have enough backbone to stand alone- even when the crowd wants to take the easy road home. A true leader cannot be dependent on companionship for his or her security, but must learn to trust in God alone."

Leslie Ludy

If I asked you to describe a leader, I'm almost certain that you would use adjectives such as strong, courageous, independent, smart, intelligent, charismatic, etc. This is usually the image that we have and has been portrayed over the years. I would even concede to the fact that many of these traits are very present in many leaders.

Be that as it may, I don't want to focus on the traits they possess at this very moment, but rather the function of a leader. The true function of a leader is to go before others or with them to show the way; to conduct or escort them along a path. Therefore, a leader is someone that simply leads by example or by taking the initiative. That means there is a potential leader in anyone including you; not just seasoned business veterans or captains of industry. A leader is someone who takes a stand, and then shows others how to stand with them.

A leader of now is someone that uses every opportunity to make a difference. A leader of now doesn't wait until everyone is listening, they speak and people begin to listen. A leader of now is a servant and is eager to assist and create value for others. A leader of now doesn't wait for an opportunity to knock, they knock opportunity's door down; then determine how they can make the door wider for others to go through.

There is much that can be said about what defines a leader of now, but we must first have a clear understanding of the role of a leader. Somehow we have created an image of a leader standing at the top of the hill alone having conquered all in their path through brute strength, intelligence and determination. However, for a leader of now, there is no such image or intention of one. A leader of now is the person brave enough to follow their dreams, cares enough to give permission for others to dream and humble enough to know they can't do it alone.

SOCIAL ENTREPRENEURSHIP

There are many academic definitions of this particular business discipline, but my personal definition is doing business with the intent of making a difference not just money. It is what I call profit-for-need instead of profit-for-greed. Therefore, social entrepreneurship is developing profit-for-need ideas, strategies, and enterprises to produce a positive social impact.

Social entrepreneurship can provide a tremendous platform and opportunities for a leader of now to utilize ingenuity and business strategies to produce sustainable change in society on the path to profitability. Social entrepreneurship is not pity or charity and is not simply philanthropy. It is, however, more than anything mission driven but it can also be attached to the free-market and capitalistic system. In short, making a profit by doing good. A business entrepreneur creates a great product and/ or service and is thereby rewarded by consumers in the form of profits. A social entrepreneur creates a great product and/or service and is rewarded in the form of societal change and profit.

These rewards are what the industry calls the double or triple bottom-lines. In socially responsible enterprises the social entrepreneur seeks to measure his or her success not only in net profits, but in the net effect their business has made in a particular area of interest or need. Double and triple bottom line accounting attempts to measure environmental as well as social performance in addition to financial performance. In other words, how does doing business impact people and affect the planet.

SOCIAL ENTERPRISE

A social enterprise or social business is a profit-for-need company driven by its social cause or mission. It provides products or services that generates sales revenue and seeks to fully recover operating costs. A social business should generate a profit and is set-up to operate like a traditional business to compete in the free-market system. However, unlike traditional businesses that seek to make a profit to only please shareholders, a social business is created to address a particular need in society and uses profit to eradicate or provide support for that need (profit-for-need). In a traditional business profits flow from the top of the pyramid of investors, owners and executives and eventually trickle down to the employees and perhaps to a cause or communities through a socially responsible give-back program. In a social business, the stakeholders at the bottom-of-the pyramid benefit as well as the shareholders and owners. Why? Because, in essence, the business was established to address a specific issue with profit being an outgrowth of doing good business, but not the sole purpose for its existence.

Social entrepreneurship is not a panacea for solving all of our social challenges. But I endorse social entrepreneurship as a major key because of its potential to enhance the way business is done and the impact is has on people, most notably the entrepreneur. At the end of the day, when it's all said and done, you want to have made a difference in someone's life. Utilizing innovation, and business acumen combined with passion for a cause can have a powerful, positive outcome in creating sustainable change in people's lives and their communities.

HELPING OUR NATIONS EMPOWERING YOUTH

In 2005, Citrix Systems Inc., invited me on a journey with them in bringing the Internet and technology to a remote village in Ghana, Africa. Through the guidance of Jo Moskowitz, Director of Corporate Citizenship, Citrix was aware and had financially supported my prior work with youth, technology and entrepreneurship; and wanted me to come up with a plan to bring students from the US and the African village together in a potential project. I had no idea how I would make this happen; in fact, I wasn't quite sure what could be accomplished if anything at all. However, Citrix was committed to creating a technology center in this remote village. So, I knew immediately, in some way, that e-commerce and the Internet would be a part of the project.

As more discussions took place, the idea of developing bee hives and honey production as a means to an alternative income to subsistent farmers emerged. In 2006, I began recruiting students to train them in social entrepreneurship to run a company that would import and sell honey produced in Agogo, Ghana, and create this international company operated and managed by students from the U.S. The revenues generated from the social business would benefit both the students in the U.S., and farmers in Agogo.

That was the general idea, sounds crazy again even as I write this. I knew at the end of the day something had to be done, and I was going to at least try to make it a reality. I started the project by recruiting students and initially only two students signed-up. One quit a week later, but Jovan Dushner who you will read about later stayed with the program. After a few more months of recruitment, we completed our first year training over 62 students in social entrepreneurship.

At that moment, I was so focused on creating a company that I lost perspective on one of the most important areas I was trying to help…the youth. My vision for the young people that completed the training was to have them create this new company and actually run the business themselves.

I simply wanted to be their true business partner and somewhat of a consultant to them. As an entrepreneur, my natural tendency was to concentrate more on making sure the business didn't fail, and that we could import honey from Africa; and all of the other logistics that are involved.

Until one day a good friend of mine, Danny Warren, founder of One Village Planet, an environmental non-profit organization came into my office and shared something so profound to me. He told me at that moment that my product was not the honey, but the young people I was trying to help become social entrepreneurs. He told me that my attention needed to be on those young people that I recruited to help change the world. Danny's words of encouragement were a blessing, and those words have helped shape the HONEY Project into what it is today.

From a single idea simply to create a social business to sell bee honey to help subsistent farmers in the rural area of Ghana, Africa, has now emerged into the HONEY Project Academy of Technology & Social Enterprise; complete with a *Global Outreach*, *xChange Missions* (not a typo) and *Invest* programs in microfinance and business incubation all designed to help communities and empower young people to impact the world. HONEY is an acronym for Helping Our Nations Empowering Youth.

I didn't initially set out to create a program or a movement; they are simply the results of taking action. In fact, none of this was my idea. It was Citrix that asked questions about what could be done with the bee honey. And it was the youth in the project that said they wanted to visit Africa to see the beehives and meet the farmers. In actuality, I'm not even the creative genius behind this very fulfilling and potentially life changing venture, but I am the one that has the passion, drive and vision.

A leader of now must have the desire to take the initiative and make things happen, they don't necessarily need to be the smartest person in the room. What opportunities are being presented to you right now? What are you waiting on? I know consensus, right? For someone to agree with you, so you can feel better about the actions you take to make a difference.

Perhaps, you're waiting on a check from someone so that you can overcome your fear of the unknown and uncertainty. Whatever the excuse, you need to put them aside and decide now, that you can do something to change the world now by simply taking action.

"Hold fast to your dreams, for without them life is a broken winged bird that cannot fly"

Langston Hughes

"Go confidently in the direction of your dreams. Live the life you have imagined."

Henry David Thoreau

2
DREAM NOW

What have you dreamed of doing or becoming some day? Do you even remember, or has it become something you have placed on the shelf behind broken promises and volumes of disappointment. Is there still a raging fire inside of you that is actively pursuing ways to make your dreams come true, or have you resided to a light amber of coals that can be extinguished at any moment. Has your expectation and hope been quenched by setback and failure, that you feel the energy to pursue your dreams is not even worth it anymore.

Well, I am here to give your permission to dream again.

There are three key components that everyone needs for dreams to become reality. Without them, all of us can simply stop dreaming and live a nightmare of a life. However, I sincerely don't believe that's the life God created us for, so let's agree to start dreaming again. But for any of us to see these dreams come to fruition we are going to need first and foremost permission. Secondly, we need an interpreter, someone that can help us articulate and manifest what's on the inside of us. And finally, we need empowerment. My purpose in giving you these three keys to realizing your dreams is so that you will be able to identify and take advantage of the benefits each element provides as you begin to dream again.

PERMISSION

Everybody needs permission to dream. In other words, someone needs to encourage you when you share that dream. You don't need permission to dream, no one has to give you that, but you do need someone that will say to you: "Yes, you can." It's amazing what those three little words can do to someone no matter how old they are, or how much success they have had. That simple permission of "Yes, You can," can make the difference between someone pursuing their dreams or resorting to move in defiance by saying: "I'll show you."

The person who says "I'll show you" didn't get permission and unfortunately, has to draw upon their own strength to forge ahead which takes a lot of energy. Not to mention, that person is moving from a negative emotional state instead of from positive reinforcement. "Yes, you can," provides the positive foundation for the dreamer to push off from, giving them the momentum they will need to overcome potential obstacles and challenges.

It's truly amazing what can be accomplished not just when you believe in yourself, but when someone else believes in you also.

"Remember, man does not live on bread alone: sometimes he needs a little buttering up." John C. Maxwell

Over the years, I have met many people that were never given permission to dream, let alone dream big. They were told things like: "You'll never amount to anything," "What's the use of trying, you'll never make it," or my favorite; "why do you want to do that, it won't work." These negative words are all designed to stop a person from dreaming. And if these people aren't supporting your dream, you certainly don't need to waste time proving them wrong.

You naturally move on until you find someone to give you permission. Whatever you do, you certainly don't stop dreaming. Even the "I'll show you" person never stopped dreaming. They either truly believed in their dreams no matter what anybody else believed, or they were driven by tremendous negativity to prove others wrong. Bottom-line…keep it moving, don't stop dreaming, and don't stop sharing your dream. Why? Because you are looking for that encouragement needed that gives you permission to endure and soar. Let me be clear at this point. You are not going around looking for constant approval, or for someone to say "yes you can," it doesn't work that way.

What I am saying is during the normal course of pursuing your dreams, the "yes you can," and permission will come, and it may be all you need to get you over that next hurdle or unforeseen circumstance. As motivational speaker and good friend, Steve Duncanson likes to put it: "when the defecation hits the oscillation." And trust me, in life and business that moment is almost a guarantee for it to happen, and during this time you are going to need all the permission and encouragement you can get just to stay in the game.

GETTING PERMISSION

I remember the day I received permission to dream with my very first company. I had the crazy idea of developing a pre-paid internet card that would allow people to shop online without credit-cards. My uncle and I were talking about the Internet and how it was going to change the way people shopped on line. This was late 90's early 2000, so at that time everyone thought the Internet would put old-fashion brick and mortar stores out of business. But my uncle asked me a very simple question, "what will people without credit cards do, how will they shop online?"

At that very moment, I decided to create a way for people without credit cards, the unbanked and anyone that wanted to protect their identities while shopping online could do so. I called it VirtuPass. I knew the idea was crazy, but I believed that it could be done. Now, to start my new company I only needed several million dollars to design the software, create a marketing campaign and get other vendors to use my pre-paid online solution. Simple right?

How was I going to get my hands on that kind of money? I didn't come from money and I certainly didn't know any venture capitalists I could call up about my new idea. But I needed to get started so I wrote a business plan and I gave my pitch to everyone that I knew trying to raise money, with mixed results of course. But I will never forget the day I got permission to dream this crazy, bodacious dream.

One day I got a call from my Godmother Ms. Erma Bell. I had no idea why she was calling, but she told me to please stop by her house for a moment. It wasn't my birthday so I knew it was important because she didn't just call out of the blue like that. I drove to her house with my mind going through scenarios trying to figure out what it could be. I decided to just brace myself for whatever this impromptu visit could mean. I rang the doorbell and she greeted me with a kiss and told me to come in and have a seat. No words yet or a hint as to why I'm there, she just went to the back room and reemerged a few minutes later and sat next to me on the couch peppered with pillows. She said: "I hear you're trying to start a new company, so I wanted you to have this. I hope it helps out." It was a check for one-hundred dollars.

My Godmother had been a retired educator for many years and didn't have much of anything to give away or invest for that matter. But with a stroke of a pen, she gave me permission to dream. Some of you might be saying it was only one hundred dollars, but to a dreamer like me it meant that I was one hundred dollars closer to launching my new company. My business partner and I went on to raise the money needed to complete the programming and launch VirtuPass into the marketplace. But I will never forget my first unlikely investor. My Godmother on a retired income whether she knows it or not, gave me permission to pursue my dream. Her investment in me meant the world to me as she basically told me that I could do it, and here is a check to help me do it. I used that positive motivation to make sure I did what I could to not let her down.

Many people have never been given permission to dream. Once upon a time, they shared a dream with someone and they didn't get that permission, so they just stop dreaming. Whether you are the person that was never given permission, or you're reading this now and you have a dream deep inside of you. I give you permission to not only dream, but to dream big. "Yes, you can do it."

THE INTERPRETER

The interpreter has a very interesting role to play in fulfilling your dreams. This is the person that comes along side of you and helps you develop what's on the inside of you. The interpreter says things like: "I can see you being this," or "I can see you doing that." But they don't stop there; they continue to say things like: "Well, have you tried to do this," or "Have you tried doing that." Oftentimes, the interpreter can see you doing something big, before you even believe it yourself.

Interpreters not only give you permission to dream, but they help you articulate your dreams. These people act as God's helpers to push you along the way once He has given you the dream. Listen, have you ever tried to share a big dream with someone and they look at you like you're crazy? They don't stop you, but they can't seem to believe what has just come out of your mouth. It only means that that person is not an interpreter. Thank God they didn't stop you, but they probably can't help you either in the way a true interpreter can.

You'll know the interpreter, because they begin to engage you with questions and you'll find yourself not being able to answer them all. That's when the interpreter begins to help you formulate the game plan on how to make that dream a reality. Don't get discouraged if the interpreter may not follow your dream or become a member of your team, because their main function is to help point out the direction you should follow. They are not there to follow you, but to guide you.

The interpreter shares wisdom from a been-there done-that kind of approach, or has some fresh, new insight that gives you that spark to say, "oh yea, I didn't think of that." Interpreters are great people because they love to see other people fulfill their dreams. Their joy comes from helping others be all they can be.

Trust me, as you begin to pursue your dreams, you won't miss interpreters along the way. They are easy to spot, but just a little hard to find at times, because they are usually dispatched to people that are actively pursuing their dreams.

EMPOWERMENT

"Authentic empowerment is the knowing that you are on purpose, doing God's work, peacefully and harmoniously."

Wayne Dyer

Empowerment is getting the opportunity to do the work. Through perseverance and commitment your dream has moved from permission, through interpretation to finally empowerment. You have been empowered to do actually what you've dreamt about doing. Someone opens a door for you, you catch a big break, your ship comes in, whatever you want to call it; the fact remains you have been empowered to do what God has placed inside of you to do.

It is truly a great feeling when that very moment happens in your life. This is why you have a dream so that this day could come. Without empowerment there is nothing but the staleness of life especially if you have never been given permission and encouragement to make your dreams come true. It's like eating you favorite dessert, but the flavor is all gone. It looked good, but there was no taste. This is what a dream without empowerment is like.

One of my favorite stories of empowerment is from the bible. There is a story about a dreamer by the name of Joseph. Joseph suffered a lot of set-backs in his life and all of them had taken place after he had a very big dream. His father and brothers laughed at his dream, his brothers threw him into a pit; then sold him off to be a slave. If that's not enough, while a slave in the foreign land of Egypt he was thrown in jail wrongfully accused of a crime he didn't commit. Joseph had hit rock bottom, all after receiving a God given dream. But an interesting thing happened to Joseph, even though he was pretty down on his lot in life, he began to interpret other people's dreams. He was no longer the dreamer but the interpreter.

So, one day two men from Pharaoh's palace joins him in jail the chief wine bearer and the chief baker, and while incarcerated both men have dreams. Joseph interprets their dreams correctly and Joseph asked the chief wine bearer to remember him and what he did for him by interpreting his dream correctly. A few years pass and the Pharaoh begins to have dreams and no one in his kingdom can interpret the dreams correctly. Finally, the chief wine bearer remembers Joseph and what he did for him while he was in jail, and tells Pharaoh of Joseph's God given ability to interpret dreams. The Pharaoh summons Joseph from jail to be brought before him. Pharaoh shares his dreams with Joseph and Joseph interprets them correctly. The Pharaoh is so impressed with Joseph's ability and talent that Joseph is then empowered to rule over all of Egypt as the second in command only to Pharaoh. Joseph was empowered by Pharaoh to fulfill his long awaited dream.

Some of you are probably saying, how was Joseph empowered to fulfill his dream by interpreting Pharaoh's dream? Well, I never shared with you what Joseph's big dream was about many years before he met Pharaoh. As a young boy, Joseph had a dream that people would bow before him including his brothers, father and mother. And in the end, Joseph had risen to become a very powerful and influential person in all of Egypt just as he dreamt it, and was able to save his father and brothers during a long drought in the land because of his powerful position.

Empowerment is not giving you something that you don't have, empowerment is not the exchange of someone that has to someone that has not. In fact, it is quite the opposite. Empowerment is allowing what is already on the inside of you the ability to operate. Let's look at it from our example of Joseph. Pharaoh did not give Joseph something he did not currently possess; Pharaoh simply empowered Joseph by making him second in command to operate in his already established God given abilities and talent. Pharaoh had recognized what Joseph was endowed with on the inside of him, and authorized him to do the work that he dreamt of doing.

Isn't that what it's all about? Having somebody entrust you with an opportunity to show what you can do. However, none of these steps are possible unless you start dreaming now. Listen, your dreams were giving to you for a reason, now what are you going to do about them?

If you take the first step, which is to put action to what you see, you will be amazed how permission, interpretation and empowerment will come into your life to help make those dreams a reality.

Now, go dream and dream big!

"A great leader's courage to fulfill his vision comes from passion, not position."

John C. Maxwell

3

PASSION NOW

What are you passionate about? What really matters to you? Is it a dream or vision that was given to you? Is there something that you would like to change? We are all passionate about something, and we all have a purpose and destiny to fulfill. True, some are greater than others, in a sense of notoriety or recognition; maybe even in financial gain. But these are not the reasons we do what we do in the first place.

If or when notoriety, recognition or financial gains come, they are a mere by-product of doing what you are passionate about. Doing something you are good at or skilled to do, is not the same as identifying and pursuing your passion. Skills are external and can easily be acquired by anyone, but your passion is internal and only you can possess it. Your passion cannot be acquired or taught in a class; it can only be transferred and caught by others through your relentless pursuit. When you add skills to your passion it is called education, however, when you add passion to your skills that is what I call living.

Passion is contagious, and it inspires others to join you or to launch out on their own search for that fire within. When you live a life not predicated on how much money you make, or the position you may hold; but with zeal to impact the world, you unknowingly empower others to break free of social constraints and real change begins to happen.

I am passionate about helping people and business. For as long as I can remember, I always wanted God to use me to do something great for others and not just for myself. I struggled, however, with this because society told me that I had to be number one. And for several years I tried to conform to this school of thought and began to seek the "things" that I regarded as being successful.

My passion for helping people was in constant conflict of what I was really pursuing and that was…"things." To complicate my dilemma, I really enjoy doing business. Every aspect of it from coming up with an idea to overcoming challenges and making the first sale. I love the process, in fact, I relish in the evolution of trying to create something awesome and meaningful. But as a business person you must make a profit for the shareholders who are not necessarily concerned about anything else but the bottom-line.

Again, my passions were in conflict because I was pursuing profits not necessarily for myself but for others. You can imagine the frustration that I felt as I was not pursuing either of my passions. I'm not helping people and business is no longer fun or enjoyable. I had started my non-profit in 2000, but I never wanted to do it full-time.

I would always do something with it on the side as a way of giving back, but the non-profit was never something I focused upon with all of my effort. I hated the notion of asking people for donations and begging for money. That was my ignorant idea of what non-profits did at the time. I still don't ask for support all that well, but I'm getting better at it as I understand the needs of those we help. I can make all the excuses that I want, the truth is, I was too afraid to pursue my passion and do it full-time.

Then one day in 2004, in Cape Town, South Africa my heart was changed, and I was released from societal pressures to live my life based upon what others measured as successful. I didn't care about those material "things" anymore, and all I wanted to do was help people. I knew that was the calling upon my life and I was really passionate about doing it.

Finally, I decided to combine my passions and do it full-time. Help people by helping them create businesses. Today, my non-profit Helping Our Nations Empowering Youth Ventures, Inc., and the HONEY Projects we create all over the world is making a difference and improving lives. Making money is sweet, but improving lives couldn't be sweeter! I thank God for blessing me with such a great opportunity, as my life is much richer and more meaningful. More than I could have ever imagined.

What did it take for me to pursue my passion? It took the courage to face my fears and break from the opinion of others, and believe I had something of value to offer this world. You're probably thinking that you're too young, you don't have the ability, you're a girl, a boy, you're poor, you're rich; I don't know what the excuse might be. I do know that fear is talking you out of pursuing your passion.

All those things that may be going through your mind are all external titles placed upon you in an effort to define and classify you. But remember, passion is the internal equity and value that you bring to the table that can't be measured or defined by others. You must decide to let go of those positions in society whether they are considered an advantage or disadvantage for you, and live a life based upon your own measurement and definition of success.

"If there is no passion in your life, then have you really lived? Find your passion, whatever it may be. Become it, and let it become you and you will find great things happen for you, to you and because of you."   T. Alan Armstrong

UNHEARD VOICES

Are you tired of your voice not being heard? Passion will give you a voice, and it can be heard and felt every time you open your mouth. Whenever you talk about what you're passionate about, others can pick up on it, and this is how doors begin to open for you. People like helping people with passion. People like working with people with passion. And people like working for people with passion.

When your passion is natural and authentic it will emanate from within you and shine as a beacon, as if to give others the ability to have a voice. Many young people have told me that the HONEY Project gave them an opportunity to have a voice and to do something that was bigger than themselves.

This is because we place an emphasis on discovering passion by allowing young people to explore possibilities and engage them in dialogue about the best solutions to overcome social challenges. Find your passion and when you speak, you will speak with conviction and your voice will no longer go unheard.

"Decide what you want, decide what you are willing to exchange for it. Establish your priorities and go to work."

H.L. Hunt

"Decision is a risk rooted in the courage of being free."

Paul Tillich

"How can I follow my heart when it's waiting around for the rest of me to make the decision?" Unknown

4
DECIDE NOW

I believe there are two types of people that truly make real change happen in life, people with vision and frustrated people. The people with vision make decisions based upon what they see, and frustrated people make decisions based upon how they feel. Vision people are moved by the future possibilities, and frustrated people are moved by current situations.

The common denominator for both types of people is that they make a decision. The person with vision is inspired by what is possible, or what can be, and begins to move towards making it a reality. On the other hand, the frustrated person has tried to live within the confines of a present reality with very little satisfaction or results, and is now compelled to change that reality in order to survive since no one else will do it.

I actually like working with frustrated people, because they have made a decision that the current situation whatever it may be is not going to cut it, and there's no turning back for them. They have already travelled down that road, and they know there's nothing back there for them.

Before we get down to the decision making process, we must first determine what type of person you are right now. You will find that at different stages of your life you will vacillate between the "visionary" and "frustrated," so don't be too concerned if you are one or the other; or perhaps both right now. It's all good!

VISION

"Dreams and visions are infused into men for their advantage and instruction." Unknown

Vision gives you the ability to look beyond current situations and focus our gaze upon something more glorious and beautiful than we could ever imagine. This is the trait that a leader of now must possess so that they can rise above the chaos and become a voice in the midst of challenging circumstances and situations. Their vision brings hope to those that witness the change in them, because they have decided to make a difference.

Vision also insulates you from pessimism, so that negativity does not become associated with your character. Therefore, you are able to speak life into your vision, instead of words that destroy.

"Frustration, although quite painful at times, is a very positive and essential part of success."   Bo Bennett

"You've done it before and you can do it now. See the positive possibilities. Redirect the substantial energy of your frustration and turn it into positive, effective, unstoppable determination."   Ralph Marston

FRUSTRATION

In this instance, I do not use frustration from a negative perspective, but as the positive motivation that produces action in a given situation. These are the people that are seeking satisfaction or fulfillment out of life. Perhaps they see something that demands attention or an unmet need, and they finally make a decision to do something about it.

Again, frustrated people have a blind determination to make a difference or to make profound changes. Think about it from a personal perspective, what did you change in your life that was possibly a negative thing hindering progress. What was the catalyst of that change? My bet, it was probably frustration. Real change only came after you were frustrated doing it a certain way with little or nothing to show for it. So, if you are frustrated about what's taking place in society, your business, your school or life; you are a prime candidate for becoming a leader of now and making profound change.

Now that, you have determined where you are located in the vision/frustration scale and what's prompting your decision, let's take a look at the decision process. There are a few things you need to decide now so that you don't lose the momentum of your decision. A decision activates mechanisms that are sometimes out of your purview and beyond your control to assist a decision that was made.

But once they are activated and functioning, you are able to ride the wave of momentum they create to bring dreams and visions to reality. Once you have decided to do something, notice how certain people, opportunities and situations begin to show up on the scene after that decision. This is important to pay attention to as it will lead to another important decision and so on and so on. Very successful leaders are well adapted at making wise and sound decisions. I hate to sound cliché, but good decision making is one of the keys to success.

Decide now:
- What are you going to do?
- Why are you doing it?
- What will be the result of you doing it?
- Who do you need around you to do it?

WHAT ARE YOU GOING TO DO?

"We started the company out of frustration with the employer that we had because we were building great stuff and there was no way that this stuff was ever going to get into the hands of the people who could use it."

John Warnock

Based upon your dreams, vision or frustration level, you must decide what you are going to do about it. Sometimes the solution comes through the dream or vision, and sometimes just the problem may be presented, but either way a plan of action must be determined to produce the desired results.

This is the beginning of your personal mission statement. "I am going to address extreme poverty," "I am going to help people read," etc. This is the "I am" declaration that starts the decision process. Don't worry about sounding selfish by saying I am, because right now at this point you and only you have decided to do something. Remember, all great achievements in society both good and bad, started with one person making the same "I am" statement.

WHY ARE YOU DOING IT?

The reasoning behind your action is important because it provides the proper motivation for your decision. So it may sound like this: "I have a dream…" "I am tired of…." "Research shows…" There is a reason why you have made the decision to do something, and in becoming a leader of now, it is important that you articulate the why. The why will shape your story as you share it with future employees, potential investors/supporters, and/or customers etc. The why gives people on the outside an opportunity to buy-in to your decision and the ability to commit psychologically on a deeper level.

WHAT WILL BE THE RESULT OF YOU DOING IT?

What are you looking to produce by your decision and efforts at the end of the day? Will the results be helpful or harmful? Can they be measured? And how will you measure them? These are just a few questions that need to be answered when it comes to the end product. Social enterprises usually have several bottom-lines or measurable outcomes. They may include profit, but almost always begins with a social mission such as helping people and/or the environment.

WHO DO YOU NEED AROUND YOU TO DO IT?

This is an area that you must be honest with yourself. In answering who do you need around you, you must first have a clear sense of what you can and can't do. In other words, you must know what you don't know. Don't try to be everything or tell yourself you are going to learn it so you can do it yourself.

This is time consuming and takes away precious opportunities for you to be working on your vision not in your vision. In the beginning of all new ventures, enterprises or organizations the one with the vision does the bulk of the work, but they must be careful to do only what they do well and then solicit assistance in the areas they don't do well.

There will be much for you to do out of necessity that are more mission critical as you will see. Therefore, having a sober accounting of your skill sets will save you valuable time, money, and ultimately that bad kind of frustration.

"Dreams, ideas, and plans not only are an escape, they give me purpose, a reason to hang on."   Unknown

"Good plans shape good decisions. That's why good planning helps to make elusive dreams come true."   Unknown

"Planning is bringing the future into the present so that you can do something about it now."   Alan Lakein

5
PLAN NOW

Every good decision needs a great plan. You will need a roadmap to follow the decision to pursue your dreams or to make a difference no matter how great or small. Get out a pen and paper right now and start writing down the ideas that come to you about your new purpose or concept. Simply list your goals, outcomes and benefits of your decision to do something impactful.

Go ahead, I'll wait....

Now that you have taken a moment to put something on paper, you can begin systematically to put them in order according to priorities and steps that will lead you to accomplishing your goals. I know that you have probably heard about short-term goals and long-term goals in the strategic planning process. And yes, those are very good tools to use in planning, perhaps we will get to those just not yet. I am more concerned about what you need to do right now to produce the results you want.

In order to activate the decision you have made to start a business, make a difference or just to be better, needs to be followed up with immediate action. In the short-term category...what do you need to do right now? Like at this very moment of reading this sentence, there should be thoughts intruding upon you about certain steps that you need to take, small adjustments to your schedule and priorities that must happen in order for that momentum to begin to thrust you forward. Listen, it is truly beneficial to your state of mind when you make those small adjustments immediately in your life. Immediate action guards you against fear and doubt, and builds confidence as well as a "you can do it" attitude.

For example, clear an area in your room for your new office space. Change the ring tone and message on your cell phone to sound more professional. How about creating a new Internet presence utilizing professional social networks and a new email address that people can pronounce or without your nickname. Making small changes like this now can make a tremendous difference.

These are little changes that won't make it on your short-term list per se, but can make a big distinction in how you feel. The decision to do something great must become your lifestyle. You must dedicate yourself to live as a leader of now; it's a lifestyle not just a catchy slogan. Therefore, as you plan now, you must look at every area of your life to make sure it lines up with the decision you have made.

John Maxwell says: *"As you begin changing your thinking, start immediately to change your behavior. Begin to act the part of the person you would like to become. Take action on your behavior. Too many people want to feel then take action. This never works."*

During the planning process, here are the categories that I want to introduce to you that you must complete that will eventually compliment and merge with your short-term and long-term action goals.

MINDSET GOALS

Without changing your thinking, the decision you have made to pursue your dream and purpose will continue to be elusive and an uphill challenge. As John Maxwell evinced, you must first change your thought process and mindset. I will not waste your time in giving you the points and keys of proper planning without us first dealing with the way you think.

What would be the point of having you armed with an above-par plan, with sub-par thoughts?

Just because you can put a plan together doesn't mean you have the mindset to execute one. What are mindset goals? These are the objectives you have identified that will help you change your present state of mind. A plan must be prepared and followed to help you think differently about yourself, your ability and the role you play in making a difference. In the beginning of the book there is a pledge, but really it's an affirmation about what you can become and do.

Come on repeat after me: "*I am a person with passion, drive and vision. I am a world changer and a leader of now. As an entrepreneur I operate at the highest level of honesty and integrity. The world's wealth is entrusted in my hands. Therefore, I use profit to provide for my needs, empower others and defend the poor.*"

Perhaps one of your mindset goals is to repeat the pledge or something like it every day. I remember when I started my first company VirtuPass, I would look in the mirror daily and say to myself: "I am a CEO, I am a CEO." Sounds silly but I did it because I had only been an employee up until that point, so I had to tell my mind that I am a CEO so that I could begin to act like one.

Only you know what stinking thinking you have suffered from until you have just decided to take action, now create a plan to change it, simple as that. The truth is, if you won't follow a plan to change the way you think you certainly won't follow a business plan or any plan to change the world, because your mindset is telling you that you can't do it. And your faulty thought foundation will always hinder your progress.

Your mindset goals should produce a can-do-it attitude and will help you see every challenge as an opportunity. Here a few tips on mindset goals:
- Repeat an affirmation each day
- Read something inspirational daily
- Speak only encouraging words throughout the day

LIFESTYLE GOALS

This is the action behind your thoughts. A mindset change will not be complete without the action to back it up. You must set goals about what you are going to do differently to line up with the decisions you've made. Your thoughts and actions must all come together and complement one another.

You should never be in a place where you have to introduce your thoughts to your actions as if they have never met or don't know one another. Your thoughts and actions should be united in the common goal of fulfilling your dreams, goals and purpose. Lifestyle goals are a compilation of movements you are going to take to change the way you act. A leader of now must act like one, and not a complainer…he or she must behave in a way that lead toward solutions and not be able to just identify problems.

With your mindset and lifestyle goals outlined, you can now compile the list that you started at the beginning of this chapter into short-term and long-term goals. What you needed to see is that the plan now process must first start with you, not the overall goal. You are the vehicle by which the new business or anything meaningful will flow from. Oftentimes, we begin the planning process by looking directly at the results and outcomes we would like produced instead of looking at the means by which those outcomes will be produced.

So your plan should look like this:

- **Mindset Goals**
- **Lifestyle Goals**
- **Short-term Goals**
- **Long-term Goals**

The first two goals should be focused on you and the more traditional goals should be focused on the actual results you are trying to produce. Remember to keep them separate and targeted. Keep your mindset and lifestyle goals about you and the short-term and long-term goals about your objective. In this type of planning process you will create a win-win for yourself. When you reach your objective, you will have been changed for the better as well.

"Action is the foundational key to all success."

Pablo Picasso

6
ACT NOW

It's time to take your dreams, decisions and plans and put them all into action. Don't wait but take action now. This is one of the hardest steps that you will have to make. Preparation is one thing, but performing is another. This is not the great Nike marketing slogan of "Just do it," that seems to suggest such simplicity. I still love that slogan by the way. However, this action is taken in careful consideration of consequences both good and bad, and the ramifications of doing nothing at all.

"Hell begins on the day when God grants us a clear vision of all that we might have achieved, of all the gifts we have wasted, of all that we might have done which we did not do."
Gian Carlo Menotti

You act because of the wonderful opportunity to fulfill a higher calling, a greater cause bigger than yourself, a chance to do something meaningful that gives you validation for the reason you were placed on this earth. You don't act because you are equipped with a great plan, but because the very next step you take leaves an imprint not only in this lifetime but in the annals of eternity.

People may forget your name, but your actions live on. When you decide to do something that really matters, to make a difference, create a great company or solve a problem, the actions that lead to such significance have a ripple effect. The positive effort and energy is transferred to others inspiring them to take up the torch as well. Thereby, you have become a leader of now by taking action now.

There is another story that I like about a young man named David. He was destined to become a great king one day, but on this particular day he was a 17 year-old boy tending to the sheep and the needs of his seven brothers. As he arrived to the camp to bring food to his older brothers, he heard something that was very disturbing. There, off in the distance, was a giant taunting and cursing the people of Israel. Now the whole army of Israel was in position to fight the Philistine army, but nobody was doing anything about this one giant named Goliath taunting an entire nation. So young David began to inquire about why no one was doing anything about this problem that was keeping an entire nation in fear. Since no one was doing anything about it, David took it upon himself to go and face the giant.

Against the warnings of his brothers and even the king of Israel, David proceeded to face the giant head on.

Young David with five stones and a sling shot only needed one shot to kill the giant and solved a problem that an entire army could not accomplish. David didn't wait for some future moment or until he was rightfully king to address the issue. He became a leader of now because of what the moment presented to him and by taking action when no one else would.

DANIELLE GRACE WARREN

By schooling and trade Danielle is an English teacher and taught college courses in New York. Fortunately for Danielle her father was involved in an NGO doing development work in Haiti and West Africa. On a chance trip with her father to Haiti she noticed the marginalization of the women there and was to say the least a little disturbed.

But the good frustration didn't hit her until she accompanied her father on a trip to West Africa in the northern region where she saw women harvesting shea nuts to earn a modest income for their families. Shea nuts, the main ingredient in the global commodity of shea butter used in many cosmetic creams and soaps. Yet, here were these women making very little for doing all the work and taking all the risk. It is estimated 45,000 women have been bitten by vipers and other poisonous snakes, which make harvesting shea nuts very dangerous for these women.

Danielle grew so frustrated by this plight she began to research all that she could about shea nut production. Driven by the fact that there was a simple solution but no one seemed to be doing anything about it, she started an NGO called One-Village Planet Women's Development Initiative and started a social business called Just Shea (www.justshea.com). The social business will sell shea butter harvested by women with the profits going to create safe harvesting techniques and also organize the women in a cooperative to increase the value of their harvesting.

Danielle didn't wait on someone else to do something about a problem that seemed important to her. By taking action, she is making a difference in the lives of those women, has become a new business owner and an advocate for equitable pay for women through her non-profit organization. Danielle has moved from the classroom to the boardroom to the remote villages in Africa and Haiti, because she decided to do something about it now.

What are the "Goliaths" in your life, or in your community? What are the giant challenges that are facing you right now that seem insurmountable? Don't let another opportunity pass you by without exploring the possibilities of achieving greatness. Don't let fear, age, geographical location, gender, educational background or any other social demographic title define your measure of success. Despite warnings from his own family members, as well as the king, David made a decision to face his Goliath. And if David never went on to be a great king, at the age of 17 he had done more than many of the soldiers that were dressed in battle array but chose not to act.

You can never imagine the places that "action" will take you. One thing is for certain, you will never be the same as the resources for you to fulfill your God given purpose and destiny are released to you in the momentum of acting now. I won't use threats or any scare tactics about waiting and putting things off until tomorrow, because I believe a positive outlook, love, and a desire to make a difference in the world are better motivators than fear could ever be.

So, don't wait. There is so much you can do to make a difference. There are suffering millions in the world that are waiting on you to defend them, support them, partner with them, and save them. My other definition for NOW is, **No One's Worthless** which includes you.

Take action! Lead now! Improve a life today!

Leaders of Now

Jovan Dushner

Wow, where do I start? Well, my name is Jovan Dushner and I am a Leader of Now. My story begins much earlier, however, I have decided to focus on an event which changed my life and molded me into the person I would become. I decided to provide emphasis on this particular event because it has shaped me as an individual and helped paved my road to personal and professional success.

One evening at my home, there was a knock at the door, then a second knock with true intent. I disregarding it and continued playing with new Christmas toys that I had received a week prior. "Are you Ms. Dushner" as I caught a glimpse at the police officers at the door. "Yeah" my mother replied, then the following moments were filled with tears and screaming as my brothers, sisters and I were being escorted to the police cars that awaited outside.

I still remember the feeling of hopelessness as the officers told me that I was going away for awhile. I mean can you imagine being uprooted from everything you have ever known, forced away from the only family you ever had and not knowing what is in store for you now. Due to my mother's drug addiction, we all were now in the custody of The Department of Children and Families (DCF).

My reaction to the transition was unwelcomed and I let all those involved know it. I picked fights with my foster families and foster brothers, I ran away for my foster home, and I was acting out in school and receiving very poor grades. I didn't care, I felt betrayed and had nothing to work for or care for anymore. While my brothers and sisters reacted in a similar fashion evident by the pattern of changing foster homes week to week, I remained with my foster family throughout the entire three years plus.

Early on I did not know it, but landing in foster care was a blessing in disguise, along with getting a foster family who really cared and never gave up on me even when times got rough. After a few months of anger and regretful behavior a time came during this whole ordeal that I took a step back, I stopped shouting, I stopped fighting, and I stopped looking at the situation though my own personal lens and how I was being affected and started to think about my mother and the situation she was faced with. In that moment, I thought about my mother. Instead of the anger that usually fogged my perception of her and how could she have let this happened to us, to a sympathetic realization of the struggle she was forced to deal with alone.

I thought about the pain and hardship she was dealing with having lost her kids and facing a drug addiction all at once, fully knowing of the possibility of losing us forever. It was probably the most selfless outlook of my life and in that moment I was present with two choices, continue to fight and be a menace knowing it only made things worse or change and join forces with my mother and provide support in a time of desperate need. I made a promise to myself that I would not trouble my mother anymore and that I would make the best of my current situation.

To this day I have never fully confided to my mother the origin of my strength. You see she always said to me that "you were the child that didn't need anyone and you were going to be ok regardless", but what she doesn't know is that watching her fight her addiction as courageous as she did and with an relentless strong will under the circumstances she faced gave me all the strength I would ever need to tackle any challenge. To give you an example of one of the ways she inspired me was when she was allowed visitation rights and she visited my foster home to give me a present for my birthday.

She gave me a card and on it read "I know things aren't what you and I would like them to be, and I know it is difficult situation we are in, however, I want you to remember one thing, it doesn't matter how hard it rains, at the end of it all there is always a beautiful rainbow, we too shall see that rainbow." After three long years the rainbow finally appeared for my family, like my mother always told me it would. She had won her battle, and her children were returned. In those three years in foster care I personally excelled at everything I did.

I went from the worse student in the whole high school to winning an award at graduation as the most improved student in the school. I also joined the soccer team and went to a championship game and joined the chorus and won signing awards. I also formed a lifelong bond with my wonderful foster family, which I have been back to see from time to time. When my mother regained custody of us, I continued with my promise that I made to myself and continued to work towards my ultimate goal of excelling at high school and going to college to earn a degree and a respectable career.

Mr. Burrell was a guest speaker at my high school class and I was intrigued by what he was talking about and wanted to participate. So, I told my teacher that I would be right back and met Mr. Burrell at his car to stress my interest and to receive his contact information so that I could follow up with him. This is the "killer instinct" that I have developed throughout my life, I see something that interest me or that I think will be a good fit for me and I go after it. I had no idea at the time that I was one of the first students to sign-up for what later became known as the HONEY Project. After my training, I worked with the HONEY Project for a little more than two years as the office manager, while attending Florida International University (FIU) of my freshman and sophomore years of college.

Today, I am in the Master's of Accounting Program at FIU. I have accepted a full-time offer with KPMG and will start with them in the winter of 2012. When Mr. Burrell approached me with the opportunity to share my story in his book "A Leader of Now," I was extremely honored. Moreover, I was excited to share an opportunity and my personal challenge to everyone that may be in need of encouragement or feel like they are not good enough or maybe it isn't the right time for them.

No matter what you're going through or situation in life, you can make a difference now, and you don't have to wait. Don't let yourself get in your own way. Society imposes emotions on people like fear of failure, but you have to fight through it, and follow your passion. For every one person that tells you that you can't or you're not good enough, tell yourself one-hundred times that you can and you are good enough. You have to believe in yourself first before anyone else does, be bold, be persistent, be a leader of now. God bless, and I want to wish personal success and health to you all.

Robert Lee Jr.

The HONEY Project has become more than just an after-school program that kept me busy on the weekends these past four years, it has opened up doors I could have never imagined, put me in business situations most people do not encounter until their mid to late thirties and has also motivated me to become a business professional.

Much of the training and hands on experience that I received from the HONEY Project, most people my age never get to experience because they work regular minimum wage jobs or find themselves doing something totally different than what they went to school for.

Life as a business professional for me started back when I was 18 years old and a senior in high school. I initially enrolled into the HONEY Project Academy as a way to spruce up my college resume, not expecting to learn all I did. I entered with a mindset that this would be another after-school program where at the end I learned little more than I already knew about being in business. I was wrong, the first day I learned two important characteristics of an entrepreneur, 1) they always carry a pen and 2) communication is vital to more than just maintaining business.

As the 12 week training quickly came to an end in the HONEY Project Academy, I found myself wanting to learn more about business and how to successfully maintain one. Although my teammates and I started a business with capital we raised ourselves, wrote checks, maintained finances, made profits, successfully liquidated the business, and paid back each and every person that brought stock in us. I was selected to join the HONEY Project soon after completing the Academy.

Upon entering the HONEY Project and graduating from High School, I and 14 other students were now a part of something that we would soon find out was bigger than ourselves, in fact the mission behind the HONEY Project is so big it's global. "Improving Lives Couldn't Be Sweeter" is the Project's tag line and the lives we were trying to make better were those of the people that lived in Agogo, Ghana.

The goal was to create a one of a kind youth ran business that profited us and most importantly the people of Agogo. We sold honey that African farmers harvested to give them a livelihood to support them and their families because most people in that village live on less than one US dollar a day. After countless networking events, business conventions, news interviews, an infinite number of meetings all to raise money for the villagers it was time to finally meet the people we dedicated the better part of a year to.

That's right we took a trip half-way around the world to West Africa. We met the farmers, their families, and the chief of the village, who helped us promote entrepreneurship among the villagers. While over there I learned life lessons and connected with people I thought I had nothing in common with but the color of my skin.

As a result of the guidance and knowledge I gained while a member of the HONEY Project I started my own video production company called Legacy Video Entertainment, LLC. This was a dream come true for me. I remember thinking what if people don't take me seriously because of my age but that thought had quickly gone astray upon getting my first piece of business mail (with my company's name on it) in the Post Office Box.

I now know what it is like to really take ownership of something and watch it grow like a child so to speak. I admit that at times owning a business can be hard work but I enjoy being able to not rely on someone else all the time as the only source of income, if finances ever become a problem in the future I can always pick up a camera and do a video shoot for a client.

The HONEY Project has taught me not to settle for the ordinary but to go over and beyond and in the end do a little bit more, because that's how you really know you've made a difference in your own life and the lives of others.

Sean Heron

The HONEY Project has truly afforded me a great number of opportunities to grow as a person, opportunities that are irreplaceable and truly precious to me. Initially, I wasn't quite sure what to expect from the project; I knew that I was going to learn about business and social entrepreneurship but had no idea where that would take me afterwards.

Now that I'm going to college and have a better idea of what it is that I want to do in life, I realize that I got the opportunity to effectively practice the business ideas that can give me an advantage in creating, marketing, and owning my own enterprise, and I also realize that ownership is the first step to full self-sufficiency and real success.

Additionally, leadership skills, teamwork, and the importance of both, were deeply impressed upon me in the HONEY Project Academy. Through observation, and eventually, experience, I came to understand what makes a good leader, appreciate the people who displayed those traits, and exercise a few of them myself, in addition to functioning as part of a cohesive unit and accomplishing things as a team that individuals could not manage to do.

The xChange mission to Ghana that the group took in 2009 was ultimately the most powerful motivator and experience that the HONEY Project presented to me. I was able to experience an entirely new environment, and witnessed a work ethic that was truly admirable.

Observing the individuals that we encountered on the trip impressed upon me the importance of being committed and focused, and helped me redefine what it meant to take my work seriously in addition to really boosting my sense of camaraderie with the team.

I am grateful that I became a member of the HONEY Project precisely because of the influences that all of these opportunities have had on me. I've been given the tools to become a leader of now, and establish myself as a competitor and collaborator in the world.

Marissa Gross

For as long as I can remember, I always knew that I wanted to make a difference in the world. In addition to sending donations, I wished to be a part of an organization that would provide me with the ability to personally implement a program that could change peoples' lives for the better. Five years ago, that dream became a reality when I tentatively entered a large classroom, completely packed with my future HONEY Project student partners, and listened as Mr. Nathan Burrell gave the presentation that would completely change my life, and the lives of people thousands of miles away in Agogo, Ghana.

My experience with the HONEY Project has instilled in me invaluable professional entrepreneurial experience while providing me with a stable foundation of business acumen and executive knowledge. My numerous duties as Vice-President of the HONEY Project allowed me to realize my full potential as a businesswoman while advocating social change through promoting sustainability and economic prosperity for the people of Agogo, Ghana On a personal level, my incredible experience with the HONEY Project permeated into my daily life by dually imbuing me with the determination, social skills, and work ethic to achieve persistent individual dreams, and by giving me the confidence to conceive of new ones.

The HONEY Project's far- reaching impact in the lives of our partners in Agogo, Ghana demonstrated to me how anyone is capable of making a difference in the lives of others. The HONEY Project's journey to Ghana in March 2009 has been the most memorable and emotional period of my life.

Specifically, the most memorable moment occurred when my mother and I interviewed six HONEY Project female Ghanaian partners in the HONEY Project office in Agogo. My personal belief in social service was affirmed and my mindset on the importance of family and community changed after listening to my partner's incredible stories of hope amidst lives of sadness and socio-economic oppression.

One similarity between every one of my partner's story was the overwhelming concept that each of them left their families behind in Northern Ghana to come to Southern Ghana and tirelessly work to support their separated families. From these powerful individuals

I learned the true meaning of self-sacrifice and dedication, as they told me the different ways they were willing to sacrifice their future to provide for their children's future. Finally, the sad and compelling stories ended when each of them women explained to me how the HONEY Project's presence in Ghana provided them with an alternative future, a better future for both themselves and their families. At that moment I realized the full impact of the HONEY Project and the meaning behind the company's motto, "Improving Lives Couldn't Be Sweeter."

Currently, I am a sophomore in college studying business and history at Columbia University. Looking back, I realize the major impact the HONEY Project has had on my life and in my life's future direction. At Columbia, I volunteer and work in the social service sector in a variety of ways, each way affecting a different social sector. In addition to being a full time student, I work to improve the living conditions of Harlem residents through my work with Community Impact, I plan events and programs for my business fraternity, and I impart the leadership knowledge I gleaned from my years as a HONEY Project partner to my fellow Columbia students through my leadership position in the Emerging Leaders Program.

My experience in the HONEY Project has impacted my college experience, both academically and socially by inspiring me to pursue a business-related career, while maintaining a commitment to improve the world around me. I attribute all of my current and future successes and opportunities to the company that has shaped me into an assured, committed social leader. I will never forget the day I hesitantly walked into a classroom, full of unfamiliar faces and ideas, and left the familiar Nova campus with a new, anomalous future as a HONEY Project partner.

Clinton Lucien-Burrell

My journey of becoming a Leader of Now started in the HONEY Project Academy by first going to the training sessions, which my mom heard about on the radio. So I went to the Academy every week not missing a class. During this training we were split into different groups where we had to work together and come up with a name and a product/service. The hard part was getting investors, not only did we have to turn a profit but we had to do it as a group.

After the training I went to an interview process in which I was selected to be part of the HONEY Project. After a while of figuring out what I was good at and what I was passionate about, I decided to be a graphic designer. So during my time in the HONEY Project I designed handouts, flyers, new logos and other tangibles.

During my time in the HONEY Project I was able to become an xChange Agent and travel to Agogo, Ghana. It was a great opportunity to meet people and not just anyone; we were able to rub elbows with the chief of Agogo, the president of Ghana and the women who actually did the harvesting. I also was able to go site seeing which was extremely fun. We went on a safari, walked across a canopy bridge, visited different high schools, went to the market and visited a couple of the other villages as well. But we weren't there to just have fun we also had to get some work done.

We checked up on the technology center that the Citrix Corporation built there which allows them to connect with the rest of the world. We were also able to harvest our own honey with farmers that we were there to help. While we were at the different schools we had a chance to talk to the students there and see what it's like in another country. Surprisingly, they were similar to me with hopes dreams and ambitions. I spoke to a group that was pretty funny and they liked to rap and listen to the same music that I like.

Now that I've started my own business called Liquid Bleu Studios which does graphic design work, I've been included in the HONEY Project Invest program. This is where young entrepreneurs can get incubation and mentoring to be better business people. This whole experience has been life changing. I've learned so many things like how to market yourself, how to work and get along with other people, also that being professional is key.

Traveling is something you don't get from a classroom it has opened my eyes and heart; the HONEY Project helped me see that there are people with voices unheard and that there is poverty all around the world. Even as a person, I have become more aware of who I am and kinder to those who ask for my help. If it weren't for the efforts of Nathan Burrell and his dedication to the HONEY Project I would still be sitting around doing nothing but playing games and wasting my talent. The HONEY Project is a great opportunity for any young entrepreneur willing to learn and ready to act now.

Rayna Lunn

When my mom told me about the HONEY Project workshops over the summer, I was reluctant to attend. I told her that I didn't want to become a business woman when I grow up. Little did I know, the HONEY project is about much more than financing and management. The HONEY Project taught me how to be a social entrepreneur and a leader of now.

I gained a sense of independence and learned how to take matters into my own hands. Mr. Burrell taught me how to write a business plan and network with other entrepreneurs. As a part of the HONEY Project, I have built strong business connections and friendships. The HONEY Project gave me an opportunity to make a social impact on others around the world. This past summer, I along with six other xChange Agents, travelled to Agogo, Ghana to spend two weeks building relationships with students who desired to become a part of the HONEY Project. When we arrived in the capital, Accra, we spent two days taking in the sights and showering with hot water.

When we arrived in Agogo, we spent the next ten days at a Pentecostal Bible college; there were no hot showers there! While the accommodations weren't five stars, I did enjoy our stay. We always had a full schedule- we met hundreds of students at two senior high schools, planted teak trees, toured fish farms, and hosted empowerment workshops with high school students.

This trip was just a start- in the summer of 2012, I plan to return and implement my business plan for Youth Teaching Youth. Youth Teaching Youth is a program for children ages 3-8 to receive primary education in Agogo, Ghana. In Ghana, high school graduates have to wait six months before attending a university.

The program will be taught by high school graduates who aspire to become teachers. Youth Teaching Youth provides high school graduates with six months of teacher experience and provides pre-school students with a jump start in their elementary education.

I believe that Youth Teaching Youth is a step in fulfilling the second UN Millennium Development Goal- to achieve universal primary education. Through the efforts of

Mr. Burrell and the HONEY Project, I believe that I can and will make and an impact on lives around the world. As Mr. Burrell says, "improving lives couldn't be sweeter!"

"Tis the business of little minds to shrink; but he whose heart is firm, and whose conscious approves his conduct, will pursue his principles unto death."
Thomas Paine

"Expedients are for the hour; principles for the ages."
Henry Ward Beecher

"There are three constants in life…change, choice and principles."
Stephen Covey

THE PRINCIPLES

Here are a few timeless principles that should be added to your Mindset and Lifestyle development goals. You will find that many of these principles apply personally, but can and should be transferred to your business, organization or endeavor to create something great. As a leader of now, you will find that there will be many temptations to take short cuts to reach your goals. But these principles will ensure you maintain a solid foundation to build upon. Trust me, you will need them and they work.

Commitment

"What you are committed to is where you will find success".
In business and life, commitment to a goal, plan or the team can make the difference in whether you experience success or not. Be committed to doing something great, improving a life and impacting the world.

Simplicity

Keep it simple. In business you don't have to prove how smart you are because you own the company. If you are profitable or solve a problem, people will automatically assume that you are smart. Therefore, keep the business model simple and don't get too complicated.

Integrity

Are you solid as a rock? Having a sure foundation is the key in standing the test of time and enduring the ups and downs of the business cycle. The law of integrity is more than mere honesty, but is more interested in the internal workings of an entrepreneur and business.

Faith

Always give God thanks and trust in Him, because starting anything that matters in essence is a leap of faith.

Risk and Reward

There is a saying that goes: the greater the risk, the greater the reward. The point we want to focus on in this law is that risk is always involved in any venture and you always expect a reward, no matter how great or small. Real successful entrepreneurs have learned over time how to minimize risk and maximize reward.

Momentum

Obtain success by utilizing the force of movement to advance your passion, ideas and your business to new heights. Momentum will allow you to overcome obstacles easier, recover from mistakes quickly and make the opportunity of impacting the world a possibility.

Honesty

This world has no place for the dishonest or untrustworthy. Customers, banks, investors and employees seek and desire to be in business with people they can trust.

Character

Spend more time developing your character than your ability and skills. No matter how great your ability and skillful you may be, nobody will really ever notice if you have terrible character. Good Character provides a clear view for others to recognize your abilities and skills.

Empowerment

Empowerment is the permission for others to access and pursue their passion, dreams and vision. It is the authorization to allow others to reveal what they already possess. Create something that will bring out the best in people.

Single Mindedness

Stay focused on your business not your competition. Seek to create value in the industry or market you operate in. Staying single minded does not mean you don't have vision. It simply means you have a made up mind to create a company of value for your customers, employees and yourself. Stick with your vision!

Sowing and Reaping

An entrepreneur should strive to be generous. They should use profits to not only increase one's own wealth or market share, but to give to the community that so generously gave to them. The entrepreneur must be the example of good corporate citizenship.

Righteousness

Always doing what is right even at a loss to your business. In business you will be tempted to cut corners and can easily justify your actions with the excuse you saved the company money. However, cutting corners weakens the foundation of your company and eventually it will not be able to stand. Always do what is right even when it hurts.

ABOUT THE PROJECT

Helping Our Nations Empowering Youth Project (HONEY Project) is an educational and economic development initiative that harnesses the passion, energy and inventiveness of the youth to address challenging global issues through social enterprise and innovation.

HONEY Projects are designed to provide positive economic opportunities while addressing the issues of poverty mitigation, sustainable development and youth empowerment. The HONEY Project is a comprehensive program that is responding to the crucial need to address global poverty alleviation by providing a unique, innovative and hands-on program for young people who are motivated and in search of enriching experiences.

We focus on the discipline of social entrepreneurship training for youth by providing invaluable real-time business experience and leadership development.

MISSION

To inspire, equip and empower young people to impact the world through social enterprise.

GOALS

- Assist in global poverty alleviation
- To create a new generation of social entrepreneurs
- Integrate technology as a fundamental tool in socio-economic development
- To implement social entrepreneurship as part of a global academic curriculum

PROGRAM INITIATIVES

The HONEY Project is comprised of 4 initiatives specifically designed to impact social issues in the areas of youth empowerment, poverty alleviation and sustainable development.

HONEY PROJECT ACADEMY

People. Passion. Planet. Profit

HONEY Project Academy of Technology and Social Enterprise provides social entrepreneurship training and real-time invaluable business experience combined with mentoring and continuing education. The academy offers several interactive and innovative training programs that provide the foundation for business success. Upon completion of the HONEY Project Academy students become "Certified Change Agents" (CCAs) where they are eligible to participate in additional HONEY Project programs and have an opportunity to start their own business.

Academy Offerings:
- *Virtual Academy*
- *Rallies Advancing Prosperity Sessions (R.A.P. Sessions)*
- *Social Business Challenge*
- *HONEY Clubs*

GLOBAL OUTREACH

HONEY Project *Global Outreach* initiative was created to address social and economic disparities in emerging nations and communities. Global Outreach provides on the ground training and support to implement poverty relief programs. Certified Change Agents will help design and implement market-based solutions to address sustainable development.

xCHANGE

HONEY Project *xChange* is a cultural and educational exchange program for young aspiring Change Agents featuring inbound and outbound missions to emerging nations. The *xChange* provides practical on-the-ground experience in global business development and sustainability.

INVEST

HONEY Project *Invest* is our microenterprise and incubator initiative. We provide microloans to young people and incubate their businesses in an effort to help them build self-sufficient companies.

Program Offerings:

- *Microfinancing*
- *Microfranchising*
- *Youth Incubator*
- *Business Mentoring*
- *Business acceleration*
- *Continuing education*

ABOUT THE AUTHOR

Nathan Burrell is a pastor, author, speaker and social innovator with unique experience in both the public and private sectors of industry. In 2000, he launched Helping Our Nations Empowering Youth Ventures, Inc. (HONEY Ventures), a non-profit organization founded to promote economic development through the effective utilization of technology and social enterprise.

In 2006, Nathan created the award-winning Helping Our Nations Empowering Youth Project (HONEY Project) to inspire, equip and empower young people to impact the world through social enterprise. In addition, he is co-founder of the HONEY Project Academy of Technology and Social Enterprise designed to implement social entrepreneurship as part of a global academic curriculum.

Nathan enjoys playing sports and is an avid reader and traveler. He loves spending time with his wife Jacquecine and four children.

Follow: @leaderofnow
Email: lead@leaderofnow.com
www.leaderofnow.com

If you are interested in conducting a HONEY Project Academy training at your local school, church or community center or hosting a R.A.P. Session please call or email us:

Visit:
Helping Our Nations Empowering Youth Project
www.honeyproject.org
info@honeyproject.org
(954) 323-6717

To apply:
HONEY Project Academy of Technology & Social Enterprise
www.honeyprojectacademy.org
(954) 323-6717
Facebook.com/Honey Project Academy

NOTES

www.ingramcontent.com/pod-product-compliance
Lightning Source LLC
LaVergne TN
LVHW051846080426
835512LV00018B/3100